NEW ORLEANS OBSERVED
drawings and observations of america's most foreign city

errol barron

FOREWORD BY JOHN H. LAWRENCE
director of museum programs, the historic new orleans collection

TULANE SCHOOL OF ARCHITECTURE

Walsworth

for
eliot · austen
enfants de la ville

Foreword

Regarding its character as a city, New Orleans is easy to talk about and hard to describe. The warp and weft of its history reside today in its people, customs, cuisine, neighborhoods, and buildings. The city is shaped by its location and forces that are both similar to and utterly different from those responsible for the particular qualities of other places. Within this setting, his home for at least half of his years, Errol Barron has taken the time to observe and create, and in that manner, comment on New Orleans's present and its past.

Barron's collection of observations in the form of drawings and watercolor paintings are not so much entries in a guide book (unless perhaps a very personal one) but a celebration and appreciation of location, expressed through unerring line, areas of color both subtle and exclamatory, and an eye that secures the typical while concealing none of the uniqueness of his subjects. The net that he casts in discovering New Orleans is a wide one, gathering in its folds both the quiet and shaded interior of a neighborhood restaurant and the sun-drenched classic revival façade of the Customs House. The sweeping arc of the Mississippi's course that gives New Orleans its nickname, is as much an attraction to him as is a roof ventilator, enlivened by some forgotten 19th-century tinsmith with a whimsical finial at its top and an ornamental apron encircling its perimeter.

Barron's vision is sure and his observations right on target. But saying that Errol Barron makes drawings is akin to saying that Drew Brees plays football. Each statement, though accurate, is minimally revealing and does nothing to distinguish each of their labors from those of many others involved in the same pursuits, but with far different results. The pages of this book, when examined, studied, and absorbed, will reward Crescent City residents—as well as those who call other places home—with a greater understanding and appreciation of this very special spot.

John H. Lawrence
Director of Museum Programs
The Historic New Orleans Collection

New Orleans

Approaching New Orleans over the lake named for Louis Phélypeaux, Comte de Pontchartrain, one has the sense of entering a fantasy world. Like the buildings of Venice, Italy, the forms of the town shimmer in the distance beyond the water, and when one descends the ramps of the overpasses into the original city, the combination of buildings and vegetation makes an indelible impression of a sanctuary – green, dense, and human.

Living in that sanctuary, however, is in itself an odd condition since the city would not exist at all were it not for its strategic location on the Mississippi River. The swampy terrain, the humid climate, the isolating marshes that turn the city into an island should have suggested an alternative location, but the engineers in France were not daunted by these impediments. They planned an administrative center, abstract and orderly, an eighteenth century version of an outpost of Imperial Rome. They could not have foreseen the growth that followed up and down the river and into the swamp that lay beyond, nor could they have foreseen how the curve of the river, not their designs, determined the city's fan of streets bewildering in their disorienting geometry. Despite its improbability, the city has survived, enduring its share of floods, storms and calamities to foster a curious attitude toward living that is both celebratory and pessimistic and to produce an exuberant architecture to be the setting for its rituals.

This book is a personal collection of observations made primarily during one four-month period while on sabbatical from the Tulane University School of Architecture (2009). Each day for several hours I would drive or ride my bicycle through the neighborhoods of the city stopping where something caught my eye. The book is loosely organized by areas – the old quarter, downtown, the center, uptown, with scattered examples of oddities. The pleasure of taking this broad view of the city, of being a tourist in my own town and looking closely at the fabric of the city through the medium of drawing was pronounced, and reflecting on what makes the city so particular very seductive.

New Orleans architecture is an architecture of public life as well as private. The proximity of buildings, the proliferation of exterior spaces (porches, galleries, verandas), the relatively mild climate seem to have nurtured a social scene that even air conditioning has not fully suppressed. Place affects behavior; the way we want to live affects the way we build. Can other cities learn from this place without resorting to pastiche and literal imitation?

Perhaps this question cannot be fully answered, but there are many lessons to be learned here not only about what makes a livable city but what values are worth having in a city in terms of density, scale, color, texture and the dangers of overvaluing the car, the commodious street, and convenience in general.

New Orleans is appealing for its contrarian embracing of the modern world. Its standards for progress and commerce may be different from those of "mainstream" America, but it gives a generous supply of alternatives that make living here an experience not found elsewhere in North America. The drawings in this book, like the city itself, are varied and improvisational. More of an homage than a guide, the collection is an effort to illustrate aspects of the city that have inspired affection, humor, and respect and to record the many trips exploring a place that defies easy description.

The drawings are taken from my sketchbooks. They are reproduced here in the same format of those books, a beautiful linen bound variety made in Paris by Sennelier, and the same size as the original books. The drawings are numbered and notes on them can be found in the back of the book from pages 119 – 122.

The book is an encouragement to wander, to slow down one's pace and look closely. New Orleans is a city that rewards such an approach because of its rich visual and sensory appeal, its relatively small size, its compactness and its strangeness. After the disastrous hurricane of 2005, when the city was almost lost, New Orleans has resurfaced. It is now recognized as a place of cultural richness and physical beauty too precious to be lost or overlooked.

Errol Barron
New Orleans   2011

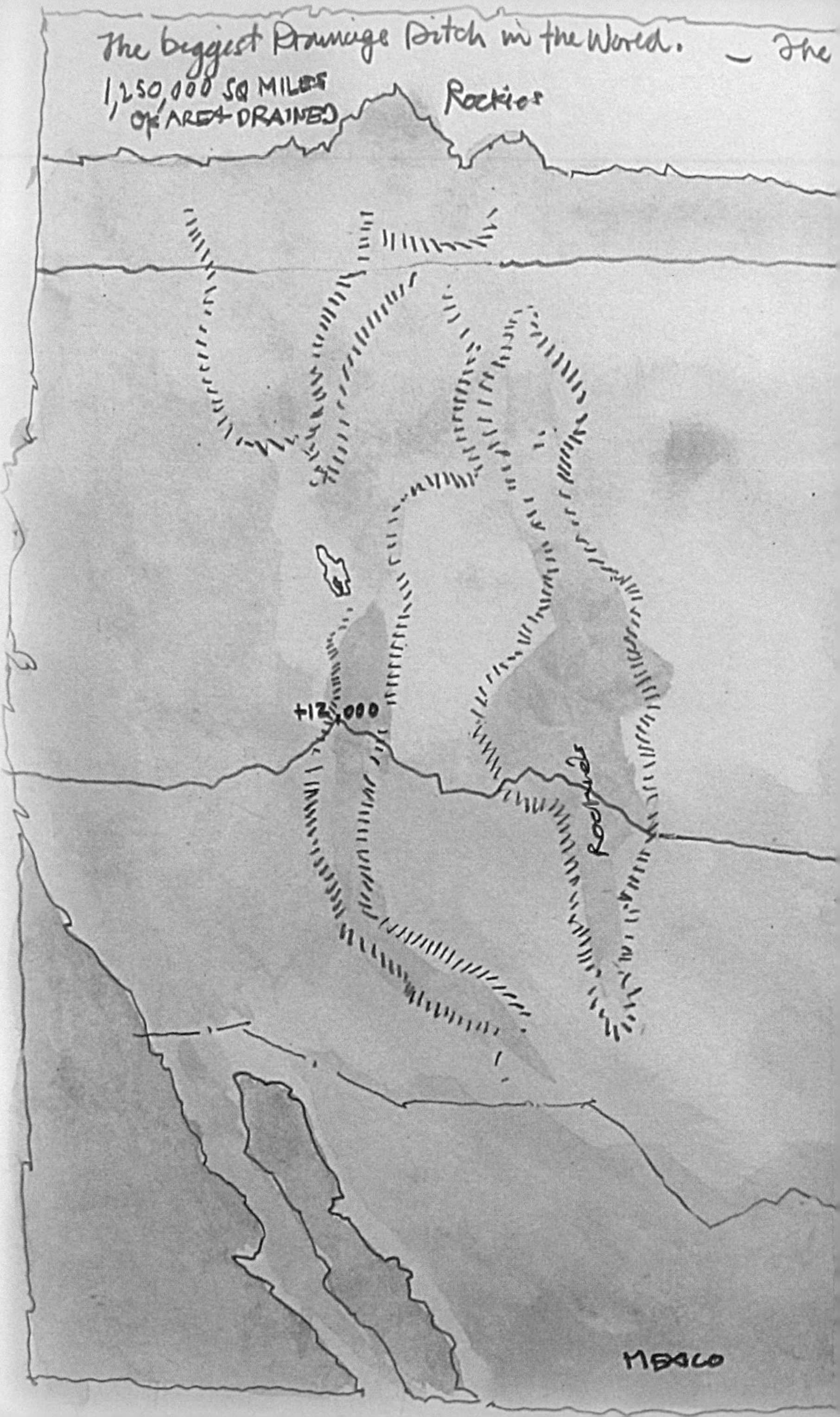

The biggest Drainage Ditch in the World. — The

1,250,000 SQ MILES
OF AREA DRAINED

Rockies

+12,000

Rockies

MEXICO

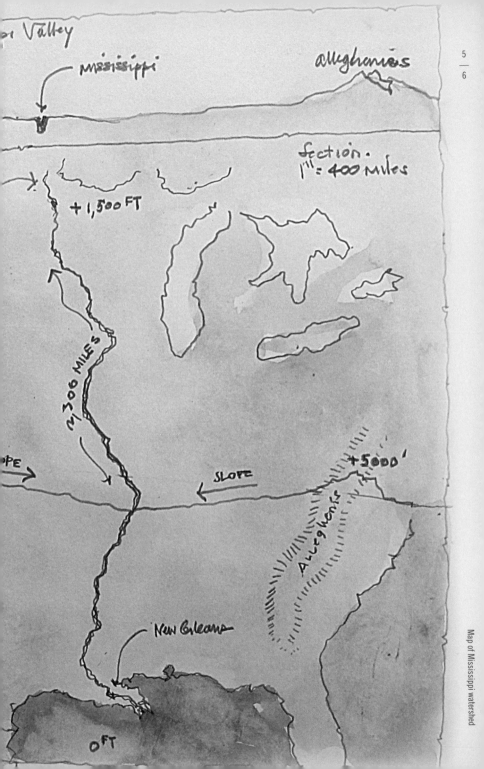

Valley

Mississippi

alleghenies

section.
1" = 400 Miles

+ 1,500 FT

2,300 MILES

SLOPE

SLOPE

+ 5000'

Alleghenies

New Orleans

0 FT

like a sponge – the land is half water – porous. 10

vulnerable — Now from 2000' above NO, you

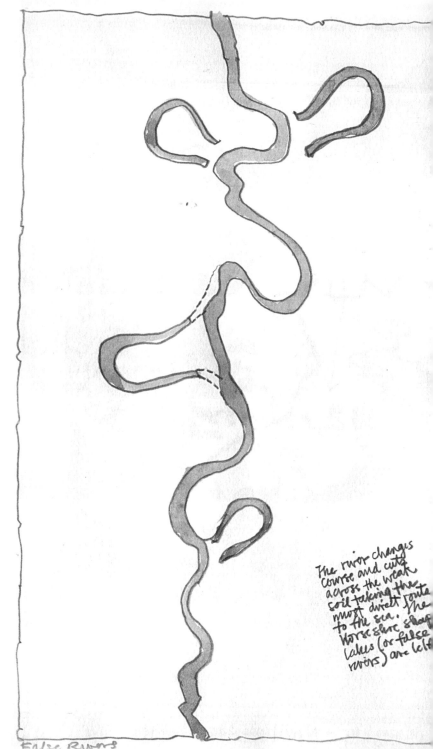

The river changes course and cuts across the weak soil taking the most direct route to the sea. The Horseshoe shaped lakes (or false rivers) are left

False Rivers

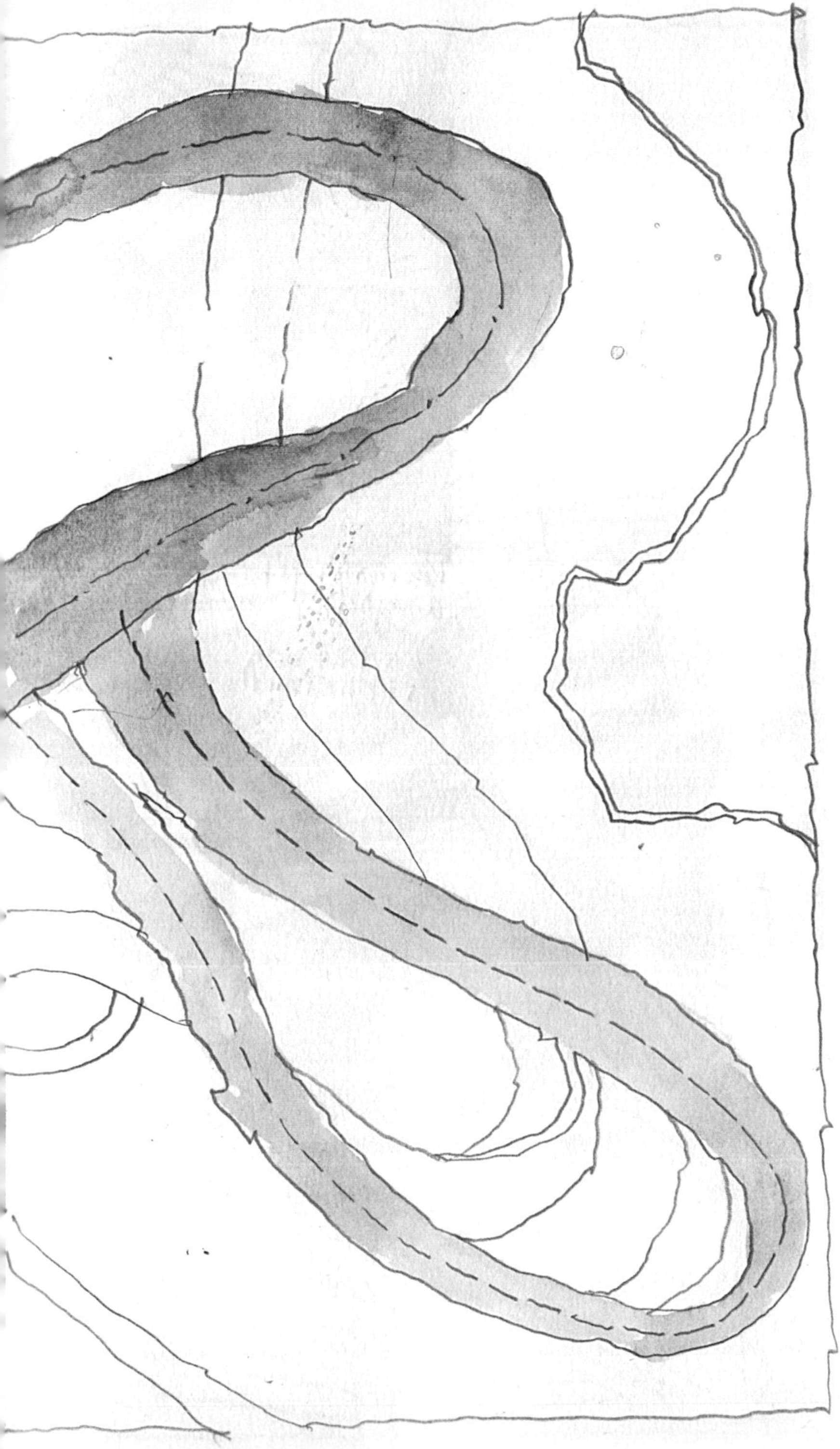

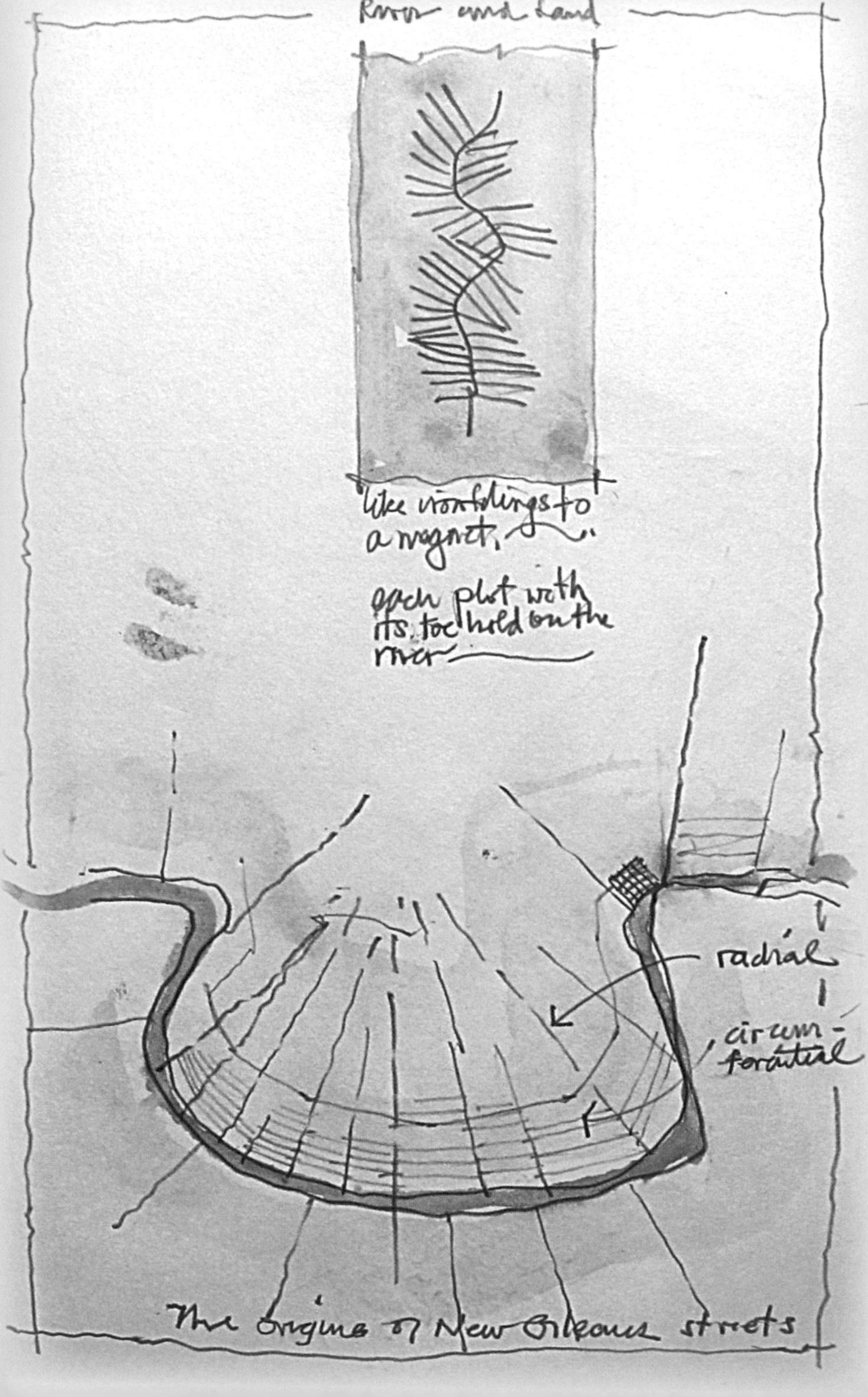

River and Land

like iron filings to
a magnet.

each plot with
its toe hold on the
river

radial

circum-
ferential

The origins of New Orleans streets

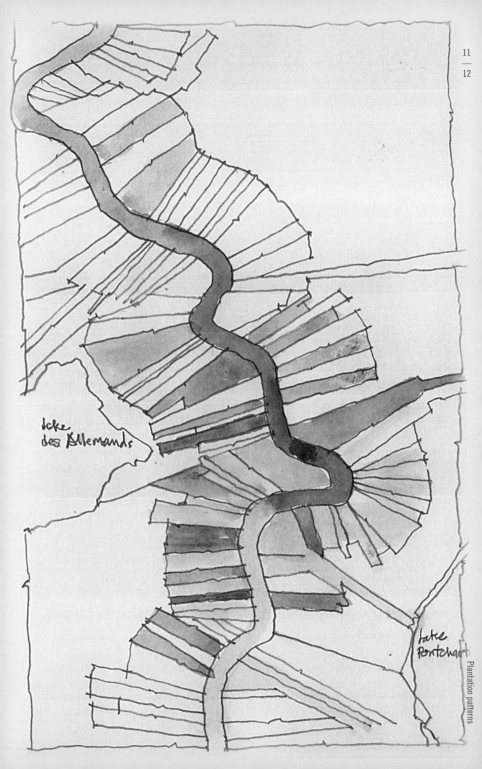

lake
des Allemands

lake
Pontchartrain

Plantation patterns

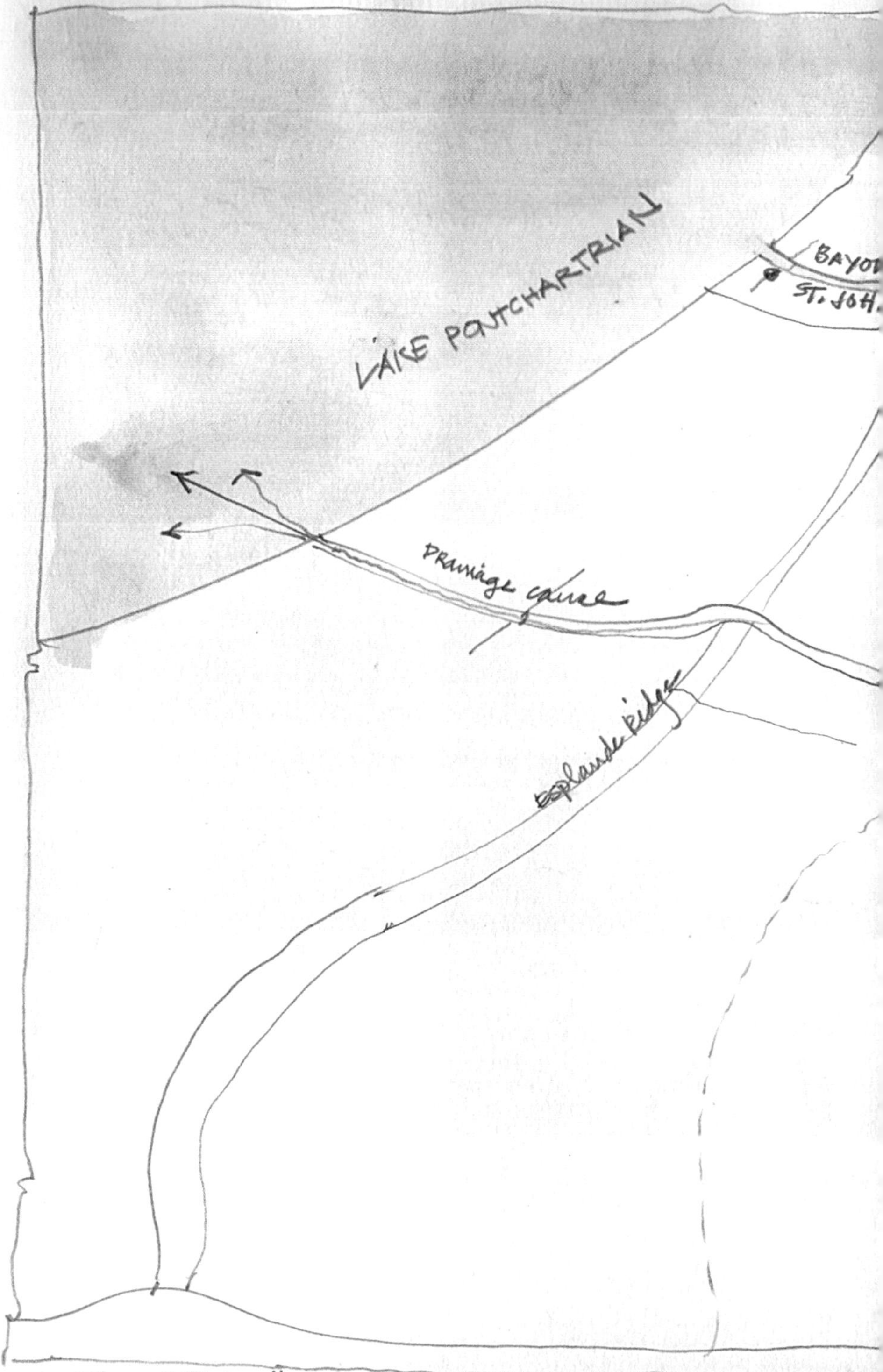

LAKE PONTCHARTRAIN

BAYOU
ST. JOH.

Drainage canal

esplanade ridge

The "BOWL" of New Orleans —

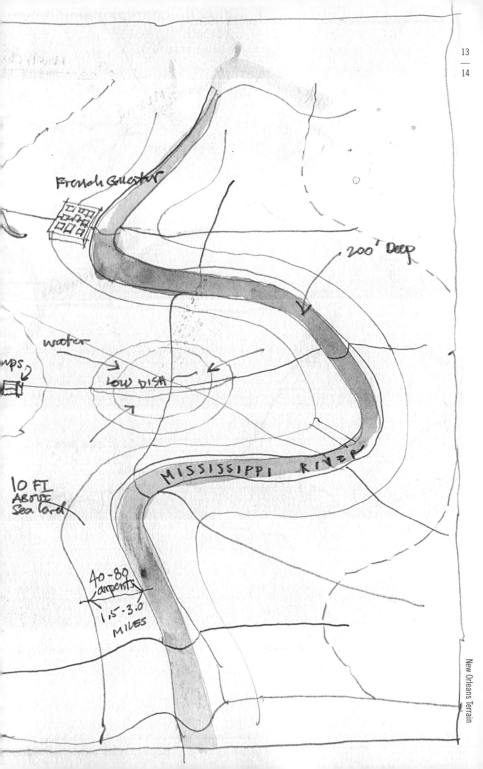

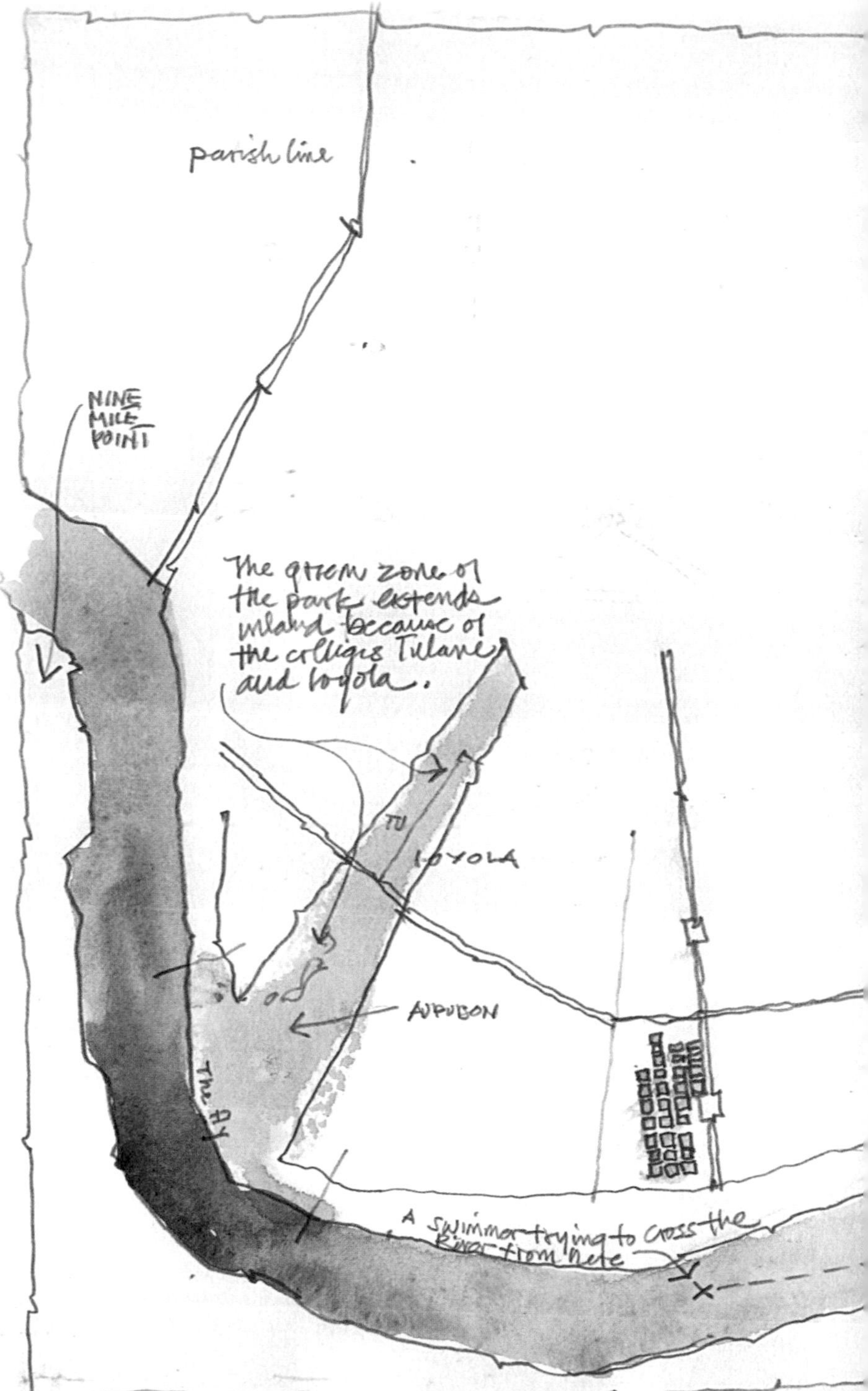

parish line

NINE MILE POINT

The green zone of the park extends inland because of the colleges Tulane and loyola.

TU

LOYOLA

The Fly

AUDUBON

A swimmer trying to cross the River from here

×

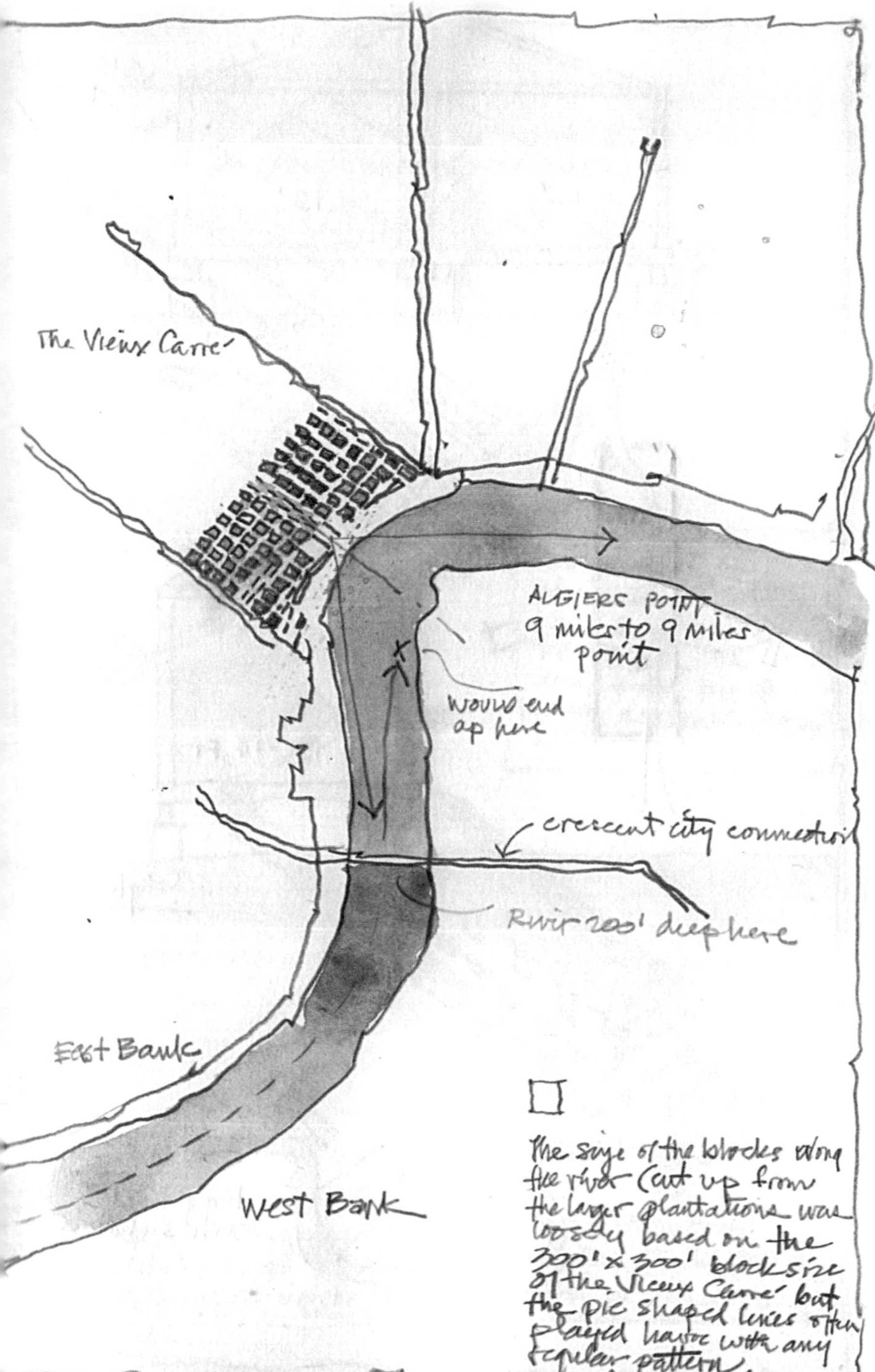

The Vieux Carré

ALGIERS POINT
9 miles to 9 miles
point

would end
up here

crescent city connection

River 200' deep here

East Bank

West Bank

The size of the blocks along
the river cut up from
the larger plantations was
loosely based on the
300' x 300' block size
of the Vieux Carré but
the pie shaped lines often
played havoc with any
regular pattern.

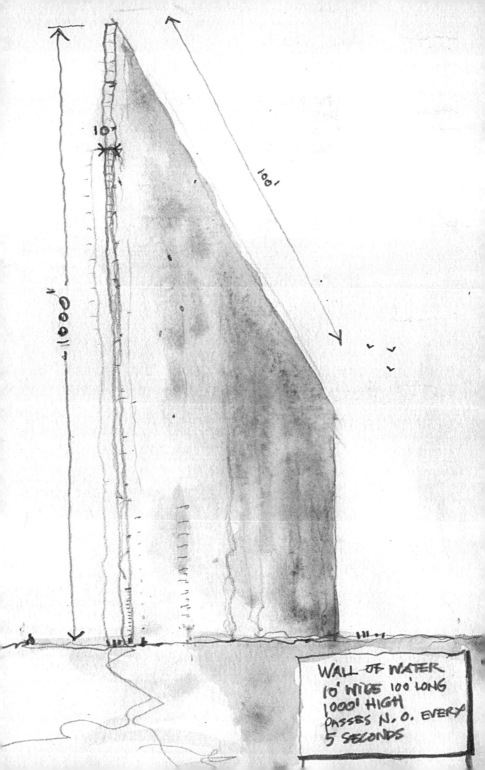

1000'

100'

10'

WALL OF WATER
10' WIDE 100' LONG
1000' HIGH
PASSES N. O. EVERY
5 SECONDS

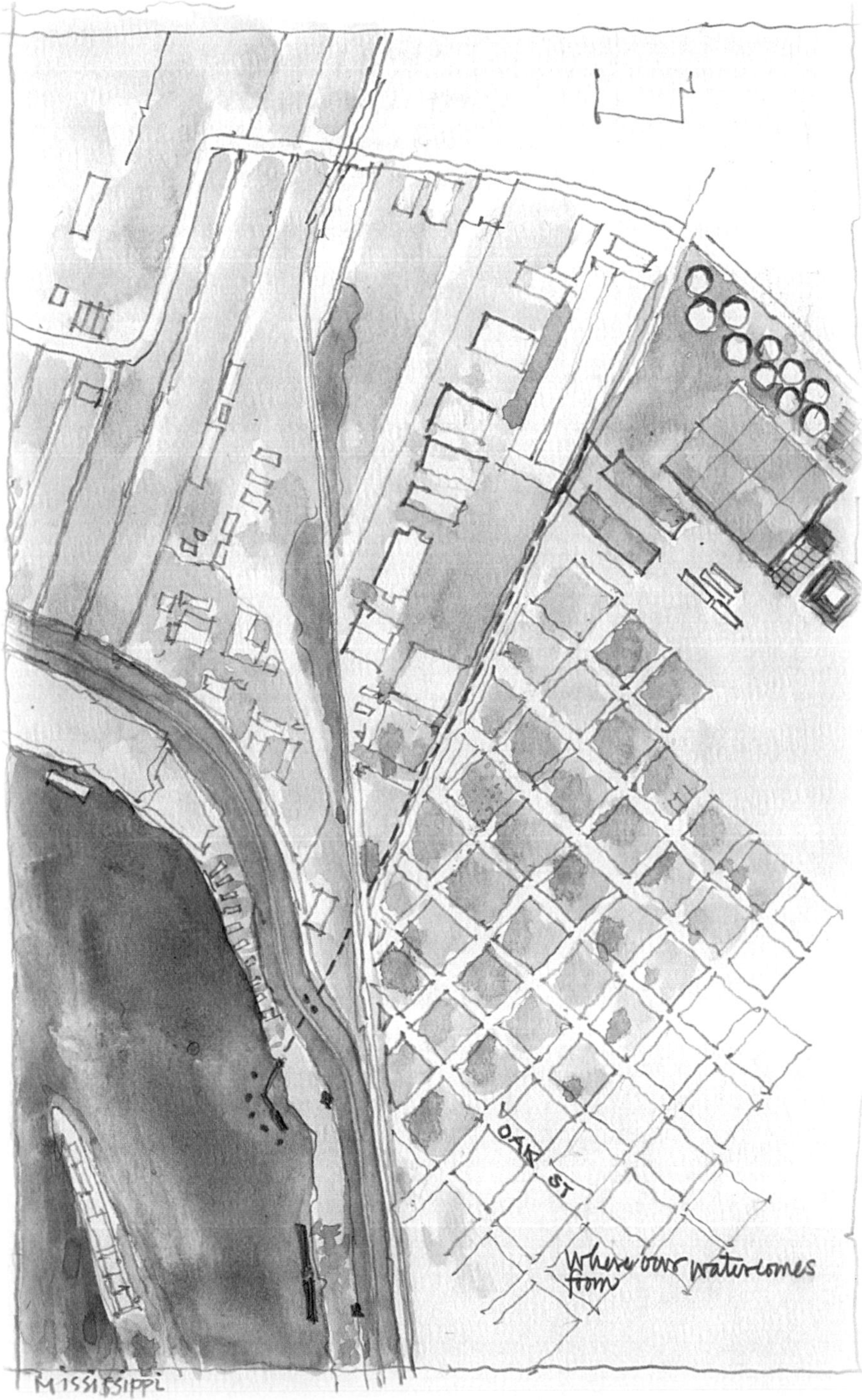

DAR ST

Where our water comes from

MISSISSIPPI

Lake Pontchartrain

Spanish Fort
guards mouth
Bayou St. John

"A"

old portage

Bayou St. John

N

"A"
c. 1930

Bayou St. John
exit to the lake

Pumping Station, Basin Street

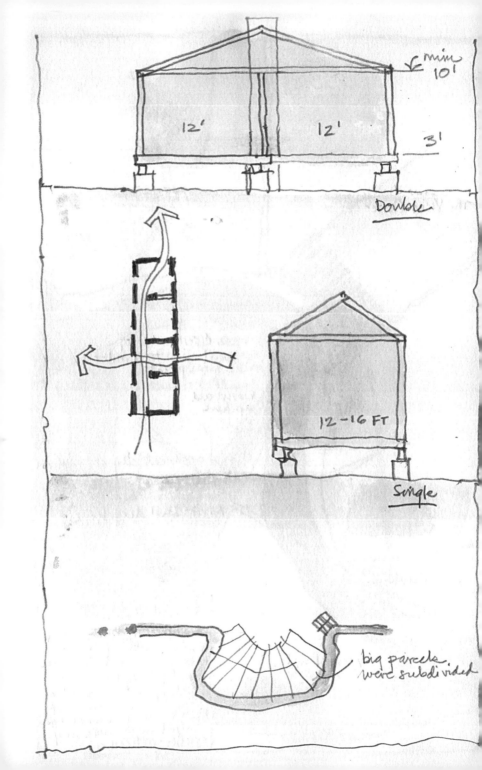

min 10'

12'   12'   3'

Double

12 - 16 FT

Single

big parcels were subdivided

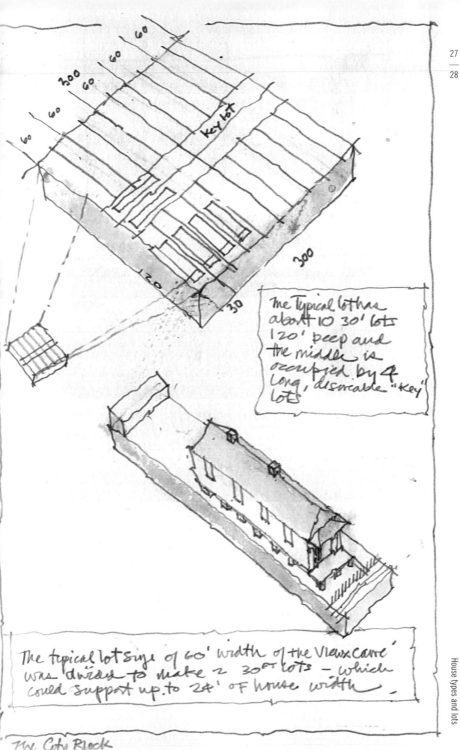

60
60
60
300
60
60
60

Key lot

120

300

30

The Typical lot has
about 10 30' lots
120' Deep and
the middle is
occupied by 4
Long, desireable "Key"
lots

The typical lot size of 60' width of the Vieux Carré
was divided to make 2 30ft lots — which
could support up to 24' of house width.

The Cote Block

View toward lake — Vieux Carré

lunch 5·24 05

518 Conti
Gottschalk
Louis Moreau

100 Royal The Granite Bldg - Quincy Granite 1838

River

Jackson Square and house with double courtyard

619 A

a

Drain

Orleans Alley — (Pirate Alley)

10·16·08

10·15·08

The Cabildo

The Customs House –

The Marble Hall ~ Custome House

coffee shop

police station

Louisiana State Bank – Bickle Hablett & Fox – arch. 1826

NEWTON - BOULEE'
DOANE - LATROBE
ASPLUND

Louisiana State Bank   Benjamin Latrobe

9
08

The portico reduced to a stair

US Mint

P.G.T. Beauregard
Fired on Fort Sumpter and
his former teacher ~ .18

St Louis Hotel
Deponille

conti

18c BLOCK
REMOVED
FOR Terracotta
Court Bedg.
White
Baroque
Blg

exchange alley

N

Courthouse in Vieux Carré

Napoleon/Grbd 1814 Hyacinthe Laclotte

1798

59/60

red

ST LOUIS
SQ.

Napoleon House
Mark Cooper's
g·g· grandfather
made the iron work
he came from Pau.

10-06

piano

only on 3rd fl.

Pedesclaux- le Monnier   636 -40 Royal   1794
@ St. Peter

funeral de "Tuba Fats"
Gallier Hall
New Orleans 1/18/04

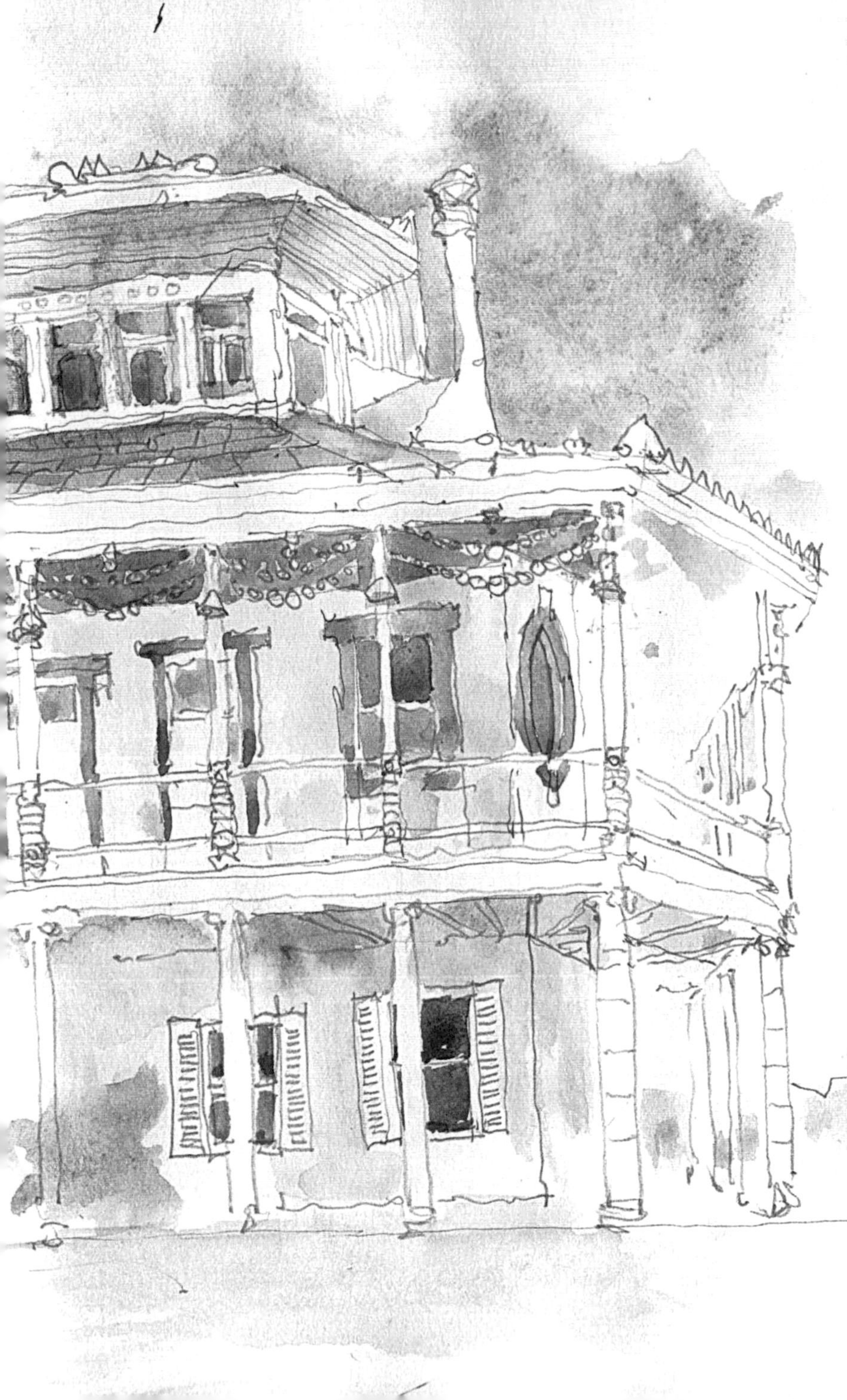

Doullot House, Lower 9th Ward

Orbean — Urbanity

John Laurence's Porch.   Marengo & Ann

WACKO CLASSICISM

Lafayette Cemetery April 2 2005

Chartres Street   The Marigny

E. Stan
Lombard Plantation

The French Market Pavillon.

EB – EMERGENCY BARRIER – The Artificial

SORAPORU

Tchoupitoulas
Soraporu St.
10·6·08

* Creole family of Color New Orleans
1700s ~ 1996

Tipitinas

· Old Dominican College ·

exposition blvd. ~ Audubon Park
houses, regardless of style and material hold a line
like eager spectators at a parade

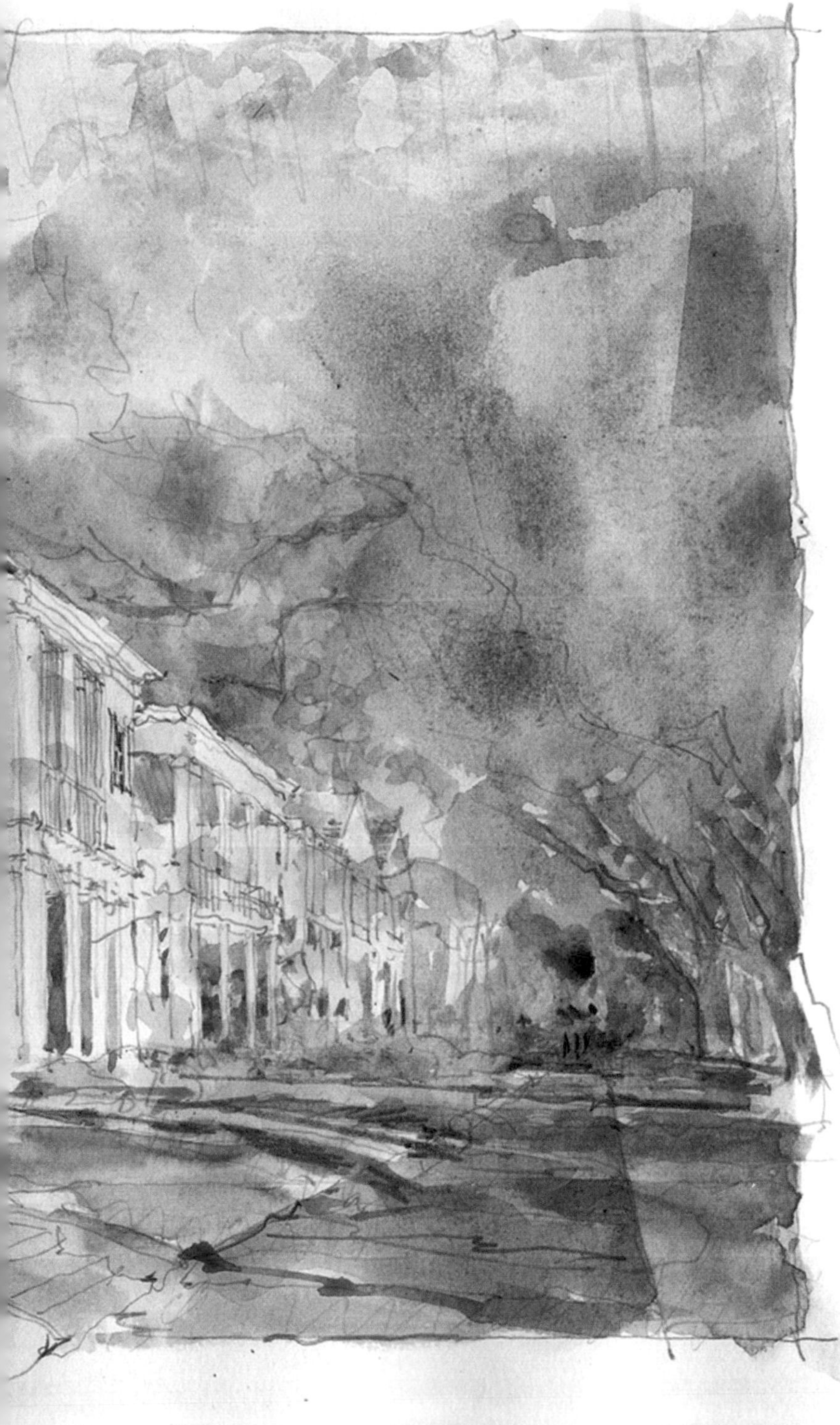

Audubon Pl.

gate

St. Charles Ave.

Zemurray/Tulane house

Audubon Place 1894

The Houses only inches apart ~

3 = 1

wall

cajun

fence
sidewalk

"The Ensemble"
4 Thresholds to the interior

THE gates of Audubon Park

Park
John Charles Olmsted

GIBSON HALL — Tulane — Andry & Bendernagle 1894

vermont
Granite

Green spaces of the sp...
of the avenue!

Loyola

ST. JOHN THE BAPTIST PARISH LIBRARY
2920 NEW HIGHWAY 51
LAPLACE, LOUISIANA 70068

Loyola

NB. The interior of
is a gaudy mixture of influences.
The pews backs and ends are
made of cast iron — open curling
in the days before air conditioning
the ends are also metal —

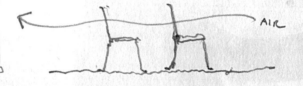

AIR

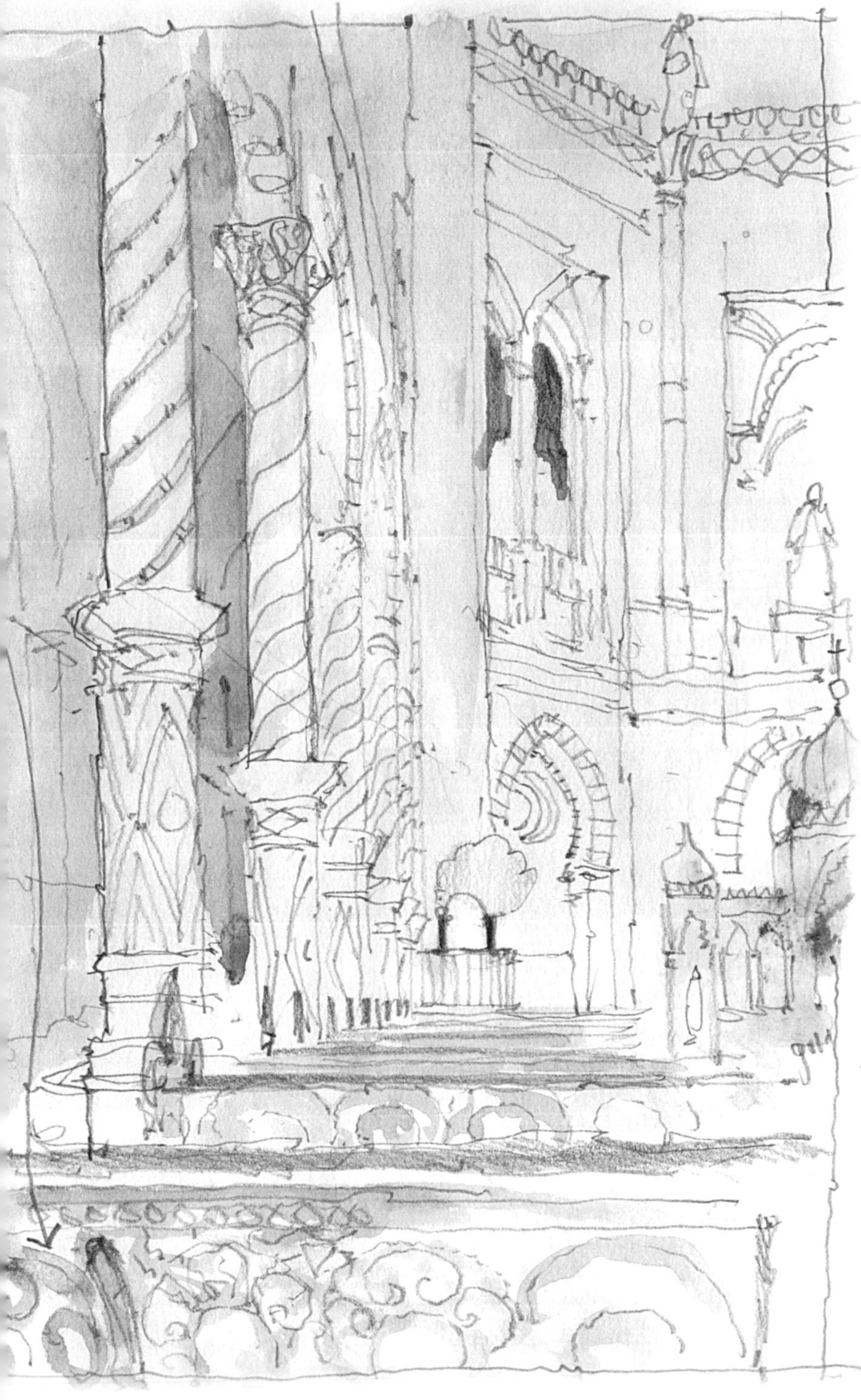

Immaculate Conception

Robinson House, Garden District

6703

old serpentine

RIVER

street

The odd jangle of buildings as the river turns.
Marginy - 2700 Block of Chartres - Sound Cafe.

property lines
follow old
estates edges

streets follow
river

RIVER

ATHLETIC CLUB

1929

New Orleans Athletic Club and Garage

a beautiful pain

Plaza Tower — The only interesting tower in 1970.

Cap

Shaft

Rotation

Base

Base

danceur
tente des gospels

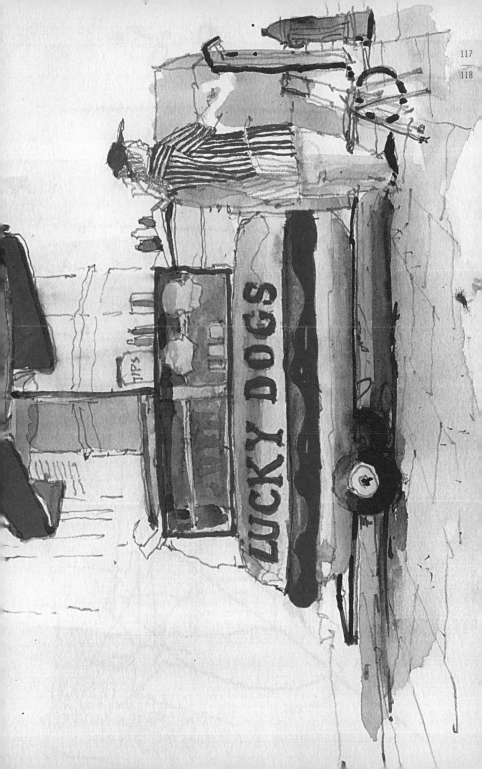

Notes on the drawings

Page 5 - 6

A map of the watershed between the Alleghenies and the Rockies that drains into the Mississippi River
and flows past New Orleans.

Page 7 - 8

The land around New Orleans lowers as it nears the Gulf of Mexico until is has the consistency of a sponge. Water lurks just below the surface and the wet clay reaches depths of 40 - 60 feet to a sand strata.

Page 9 - 10

The course of the Mississippi is changeful, unstable. All along its southern course are remnants of where the river has been. Its instability contributes to the uncertain and fragile personality of the city itself.

Page 11 - 12

Farms, plantations and all commerce required a connection to the river, so long narrow strips of land fan out along the banks and stretch back into the swampy land beyond.

Page 13 - 14

New Orleans itself is located on one of the great bends in the river and occupies a bowl of space that is prone to flooding. Land along the river is high but, in the middle of the bowl, dangerously low.

Page 15 - 16

A diagram of the city showing some of its major components.

Page 17 - 18

A diagram of the water treatment plant near the fresh water intake of the river. 90% of the drinking water enters the city (see dotted line) here and is pumped to the central treatment plant, then distributed to the city. Rumored to have passed through 6 people on its way to the sea, the water is famed for its good taste.

Page 19 - 20

What is left of the Spanish Fort that guarded the inlet of Bayou St. John. This bayou was used as a main, if back door, entry into the city.

Page 21 - 22

Where the Bayou St. John enters Lake Pontchartrain.

Page 23 - 24

A central pumping station building. These buildings, loosely based on Italian models, were part of the water treatment system dating from 1879.

Page 25 - 26

Satellite pumping station pavilions.

Page 27 - 28

The city is largely made of narrow wooden houses which, because they are built close together, give the appearance of a much greater density.

Page 29 - 30

View of the original city from the roof of the Royal Orleans Hotel, looking east.

Page 31 - 32

View of the Vieux Carré looking east.

Page 33 - 34

Early 19c buildings built on the attached, European, model, not detached and suburban. Page 33 shows one of the houses lived in by Louis Moreau Gottschalk, the American Chopin. As with so many historic places in the city, there is no marker.

Page 35 - 36

The original square and the urban buildings that make up the Vieux Carré. No other American city has such urban density or such a European quality to its places and building patterns as in the old city.

Page 37 - 38

The Armory (behind the Cabildo) designed by James Dakin. The severe style looks like an armory but was part of a revival of interest in romantic, monumental structures recalling the ancient past. Page 38 shows the most urban space in the city, Pirate Alley (Orleans Alley) five times as high as it is wide.

Page 39 - 40

The Cabildo and the Cathedral - the grand center of the old city. These buildings are stucco but made to look like stone, they create a powerful edge to the Place d'Armes (Jackson Square). The roofs and dormers of the Cabildo and Presbytere on either side of the cathedral were added by the Baroness Pontalba to improve the proportions of the square, itself loosely based on the Place des Voges in Paris.

Page 41 - 42
The Cathedral, technically a minor basilica, is a jumble of parts and pieces looking to some as though made of cake and icing. The spires were originally open wrought iron.

Page 43 - 44
The interior of the church, the epicenter of Catholic New Orleans is shown here during a concert of the St. Louis Cathedral Choir.

Page 45 - 46
The porch of the Cabildo

Page 47 - 48
Two versions of the grand entry as an urban gesture. The Customs House by James Dakin, on the left, and 524 Esplanade on the right, have entrances that are at the scale of the street, a civic scale not a domestic one.

Page 49 - 50
The interior of the Customs House. The finest, or one of the finest, rooms in the city, this "marble hall" is a combination of fine materials, good workmanship and mysterious lighting that evokes of ancient Rome.

Page 51 - 52
This monumental building now houses the police department and the Vieux Carré Commission, one of the oldest preservation organizations in the U.S. It is probably the only police department building in the U.S. with a garden for coffee drinkers.

Page 53 - 54
The distinguished building by Benjamin Latrobe, now called "Latrobe's". Originally the Louisiana Bank Building, it is a masterpiece of precise geometry used to produce a complex interior and a stately exterior. It has direct antecedents in the revolutionary architecture of 18c France.

Page 55 - 56
Never underestimate the importance of the front porch. From grand gestures like the Old U.S. Mint (1835), which quote from the Italian architect Andrea Palladio, to the operatic entry of a modest bungalow in Mid City, formality is taken seriously.

Page 57 - 58
The Louisiana Supreme Court Building (1908) was built requiring the demolition of an entire block of 18th and early 19th c buildings. The resulting confection is an anomaly of white terra-cotta in a brick city and is like a huge hot air balloon landed in the center of town.

Page 59 - 60
The Girod Mansion, now called the Napoleon House, is a grand, well proportioned town house with fine rooms upstairs and now a popular bar downstairs. The classical music always playing is a welcome relief from the tourist jazz. Napoleon was offered this house as a refuge according to legend.

Page 61 - 62
The interior of the Napoleon House Bar. Once a retreat for the intelligentsia, it is now given over largely to tourists.

Page 63 - 64
The interior of the Ogden Museum of Southern Art. The first new museum built in the city since the 1930s, its grand hall makes an off street living room where music events are held weekly. The exterior functions like a big lantern to the street outside.

Page 65 - 66
The first New Orleans "sky scraper" is only 4 floors high but in the Vieux Carré it must have seemed tall. Begun in 1794 by Pedesclaux, it has an oval room on the corner of the 3rd floor and epitomizes the French ideal of a placid unrevealing exterior with a luxurious, voluptuous, interior.

Page 67 - 68
Gallier Hall (the old City Hall). On Lafayette Square it also harkens back to the architecture of revolutionary France with its exclusion of fanciful detail and its austere classicism. This drawing was made during the funeral procession of "Tuba Fats," a popular jazz tuba player.

Page 69 - 70
The impulse to celebrate is compulsive. In this house and its twin nearby, a river boat captain, who had seen the Golden Pavilion from Japan at the 1903 St. Louis Fair, mixed its influence with that of the steam boats he piloted.

Page 71 - 72
Orleans Street. It is the only street in the Vieux Carré that is wider than the standard street. It is aligned with the Cathedral, the square and the river, linking

Religion, State, Planning and Patronage in a single gesture of city planning.

Page 73 - 74
The public life is maintained by porches and other covered private spaces, those outside rooms elevated like viewing boxes over the street. Not only places for viewing the public spectacle below, they provided opportunity for almost absurd efforts to add a classicizing gesture to link the daily world with the classical past.

Page 75 - 76
Cities of the Dead. The high water table forces above ground burial plots and provides an opportunity to make the celebration of community life visible and memorable, even in death.

Page 77 - 78
The density of the Vieux Carré is relaxed but still evident in the faubourgs (false cities or suburbs). Their gritty urban character makes these down river sites ideal for the burgeoning community of artists.

Page 79 - 80
As in most of the old sections of the city, the unseen river is present through the visible tops of huge ships that loom over the streets.

Page 81 - 82
The French Market. Given architectural significance by its oversized and monumental columns, this market has had its stalls of produce replaced by trinkets.

Page 83 - 84
Tchoupitoulas Street. The 18c dockland passage is named after the tribe of Indians displaced by encroaching immigrants. The curving road that provides access to all the docks is protected by Emergency Barriers (EB) in case of flooding.

Page 85 - 86
On Tchoupitoulas Street there are many seedy bars none more highly regarded than Tipitina's, a music venue of legendary stature.

Page 87 - 88
St. Mary's Dominican College for Women was founded in 1910 as part of the expansion of the city along the new rail lines (street cars). The building of the college is now part of Loyola University.

Page 89 - 90
Audubon Park was also part of this expansion. Created in the late 1800s, it was designed by

Charles Olmsted, the nephew of the designer of Central Park in New York. The freestanding houses that line the park are built so close together they act as a wall of enclosure.

Page 91 - 92
New Orleans' premier gated community. Texas developers purchased enough land in 1893 for a wide street and big houses, then sold off the lots and erected imposing gates to guard the private street.

Page 93 - 94
The linking of individual houses into what appears to be a single monumental row of columns relates to the strong desire for urban uniformity and civic gesture so different from the more common American model of the country house on its own parcel of land no matter how small or insignificant. Here fairly ordinary houses make a big statement.

Page 95 - 96
Individual mansions exist in abundance in the Garden District. The Bullitt House shown in this drawing not only seeks a suburban independence but moral rectitude through its Gothic decoration. The belief in the moral rightness of the Gothic style was promoted by the Englishman John Ruskin and the American Andrew Jackson Downing and used freely by governments and universities as well.

Page 97 - 98
The New Audubon Park needed an entrance. These handsome pylons form a civic entrance to the park and visually connect the park to Tulane University across the street. The two, park and university, form a green space from the river two and one half miles into the city.

Page 99 - 100
Tulane University was a gift from a wealthy cotton broker (Paul Tulane) from Princeton, New Jersey. The foresight to link the university to the park was an important civic gesture.

Page 101 - 102
Loyola University, adjacent to Tulane, adds to the rich urban mix of park and city. The two universities are
home to 15,000 - 20.000 students and faculty and are the largest employers in the city.

Page 103 - 104
Immaculate Conception Church combines influences as diverse as the Middle East, Venice, Rome and

local climate concerns such as open metal pew backs to promote air circulation. Designed by a Jesuit priest (J. Cambiaso S.J.), this stylistic and sumptuous bit of exotica was rebuilt in 1929 after a disastrous fire.

Page 105 - 106
Architectural extravagance was made possible by wealth created by shipping and the great plant, cotton.

Page 107 - 108
Many houses in the city are not square to the street. This skewed relationship is a result of the way the lot lines radiate from the river and are not at right angles to the streets. The city streets have the appearance of a grid but are really a fan shape.

Page 109 - 110
Examples of radical modernism are rare. In general the city is leery of modern architecture and prefers its traditional buildings. To some extent this profound conservatism, so frustrating to architects, has protected the existing fabric of buildings. Urban renewal did not decimate the city. Here a minimalist garage sits next to the neoclassical New Orleans Athletic Club.

Page 111 - 112
A few forays into the modern city exist such as the Plaza Tower, the first real high rise in the city. Built in the 1960s, it sits on 200 foot long pilings that never hit anything solid. They resist the weight of the building through the friction of the piling and the earth. While roundly despised, the building has much more interest than a pure box tower because of its adjustments to the context of streets and buildings and its humorous top floor.

Page 113 - 114
One of the greatest "buildings" in the city, and it moves. The street car was part of an extensive system of cheap, energy efficient transportation done in by the tire and gasoline companies who wanted a switch to buses and cars. The languorous ride along St. Charles Avenue is marked a gentle pull of centrifugal force caused by the curve of the street following the river.

Page 115 - 116
Dancer at Jazz Fest

Page 117 - 118
The Lucky Dog cart in Jackson square

photo: Karen Drechsler

Biography

Errol Barron FAIA was born in Alexandria, Louisiana, and has lived in New Orleans since 1976. He is Favrot Professor of Architecture at Tulane University where he teaches design and drawing and is a practicing architect. His office, Errol Barron / Michael Toups Architects designed the Ogden Museum of Southern Art and a number of other buildings in the region and abroad. He is a Fellow in the American Institute of Architects and is the winner of the Gabriel Prize. In 2012 he was awarded the Medal of Honor by the Louisiana Architects Association of the American Institute of Architects for his *"significant and enduring contribution to the advancement of architecture and his inspiring influence on the architects of Louisiana."* He has lectured widely on the topics of design and art and is committed to the integration of the allied arts of painting, music, and drawing into the world of architectural design and thinking.

In over 30 years of teaching architecture in the city, he has developed a fondness for the city and an appreciation of its sometimes maddeningly frustrating characteristics. Over time however, what appeared sometimes as faults now seem like assets, and he believes that the city provides a real if complicated alternative to an increasingly homogenized American urban landscape.

What could this old and quirky city have to offer to the world of chain stores, strip malls, and McMansions and suburban sprawl ? What lessons from studying the city in the context of practicing and teaching architecture might be learned ? What New Orleans has that makes it a difficult city to copy is its history, its distant but still relevant French sensibilities and its vibrant, hard to explain civic spirit.

Acknowledgements

The city of New Orleans offers a rare chance in America to study and teach architecture in an environment that is a rich hybrid of the modern and the old. It is the only extant 18th century French city left in North America, Montreal and Detroit having been radically changed, and even if the original district is now just a small part of the overall metropolitan area, its influence creeps into the city fabric in subtle ways. So thanks must go to New Orleans itself, a fascinating laboratory of physical delights, an alternative to an American urbanism often radically undermined by freewheeling economics. It has been a joy to live and teach in this city and to try to learn from it.

This book would not have been possible without having the time to wander the city and draw – an opportunity made possible by the Tulane University School of Architecture, Ken Schwartz, Dean. Through an innovative program established by Dean Schwartz, called the Dean's Fund for Excellence, and the university's sabbatical program, this project became possible.

I have had the good fortune to become friends with many New Orleanians, one of whom is John H. Lawrence, Director of Programs at the Historic New Orleans Collection. A native of the city, he is the author of numerous scholarly books and many insightful exhibitions at the Collection. His advice about this project was very helpful and his foreword to the book, a touching introduction. His contribution is especially meaningful to me as his father, John W. Lawrence, was Dean of the Tulane University School of Architecture from 1959 – 1971 when I was a student. Dean Lawrence's kind and perceptive mentoring of our generation is still felt today as we try to find ways of reconciling modernity with the examples of the past.

I also thank my wife, Kate, whose career as a teacher and museum educator has been a model of inspired learning and helping others and from whom I have learned more than from anyone else. Her support of this project, her wise editorial guidance, and humor have been essential to keep my natural tendency to digress under control.

Lastly, I am most indebted to a close friend for his encouragement to complete this project. Our friendship, based on a number of shared interests and concerns, has amounted to a collaboration over time on a wide range of topics - reading, drawing and painting, architecture, travel, craft, photography, and Louisiana oddities. It is a rare week that does not entail a spirited conversation about one of these topics, and his interest in the world, his love and joy of learning have been an inspiration to me for nearly 50 years. Without his persistent and insistent urging, this book on one of our favorite cities would not and could not have happened.

Errol Barron
New Orleans

Third Printing
ISBN: 978-0-615-55373-3

Design: Philip Collier Designs, Inc., New Orleans/ Errol Barron
Cover Design: Dean Cavalier
Printing: Walsworth Publishing Company, Marceline Mo.
Type: Trade Gothic Condensed

 TULANE SCHOOL OF ARCHITECTURE

 Walsworth